No Sacerdotalism!

Down the centuries, the laying on of hands has made a huge contribution to the fostering of the great evil of sacramentalism. While most of today's evangelical and Reformed churches have a low view of ordination coupled with the laying on of hands, nevertheless, sacramentalism is never far removed from the procedure – even in those churches. And as always, it is what people in the pew think – not what the theologians tell them to think. And, never forget, when we find sacramentalism, sacerdotalism is never far behind.

This book is no ivory-tower study. Sacramentalism and a return to the Fathers is on the march, and in the most surprising of quarters. The laying on of hands, therefore, unless properly weighed in the balances according to Scripture, may yet mistakenly come to play a very important role in the churches in the not-too-distant future. It may yet assume its full sacramental – not to say, sacerdotal – dress even in some of today's most 'orthodox' of evangelical or Reformed churches. Already, where the rite is used, it is regarded as the pinnacle of the ordination service. Consequently, in this book, David Gay gets to grips with something which is far from trivial.

OTHER BOOKS BY THE SAME AUTHOR

UNDER DAVID GAY
Voyage to Freedom
Dutch: Reis naar de vrijheid
Christians Grow Old
Italian: I credenti invecchiano
Battle for the Church (First Edition)

UNDER DAVID H.J.GAY
*The Gospel Offer **is** Free (First and Second Editions)*
Particular Redemption and the Free Offer
Infant Baptism Tested
Septimus Sears: A Victorian Injustice and Its Aftermath
Baptist Sacramentalism: A Warning to Baptists
Battle for the Church (Second Edition)
The Priesthood of All Believers
John Colet: A Preacher to Be Reckoned With
The Pastor: Does He Exist?
Christ is All: No Sanctification by the Law
*Conversion Ruined: The New Perspective and
the Conversion of Sinners*

ALL BOOKS BY DAVID H.J.GAY ARE ALSO ON KINDLE

No Sacerdotalism!

A critique of the laying on of hands in ordination

David H.J.Gay

BRACHUS

BRACHUS 2013
davidhjgay@googlemail.com

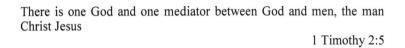

There is one God and one mediator between God and men, the man Christ Jesus

1 Timothy 2:5

Contents

Preamble

Sacramentalists believe that, under certain circumstances, spiritual grace is conveyed (or made effective) by an outward act. For instance, they believe that when water is applied to someone, something spiritual and inward happens to that person; that person receives grace, is regenerated, or whatever. Again, sacramentalists believe that by eating bread and drinking wine they receive the actual body and blood of Christ. And so on.

Sacerdotalists believe that certain men have the ability, the gift, the power and the right to administer the actions in question, and thereby convey the grace, the gift or whatever inherent in those actions. Naturally, therefore, they happily delegate vital parts of their religion – even their spiritual life – into the hands of these men, who, they believe, because they have been consecrated or ordained, are better able, more qualified to carry it out for them. In such a system, worship and spiritual service is a specialised task best left to a special class – priests – who do it on behalf of the rest. Hence arose the unbiblical notion of the clergy and the laity – with all its attendant and well-documented curses of priestcraft.

Sacramentalism and sacerdotalism are intimately connected. The former leads to the latter. If I may borrow a self-explanatory phrase from Applied Mathematics: sacramentalism is a state of 'unstable equilibrium' – it doesn't take much to dislodge it!

The new covenant gives no warrant for either sacramentalism or sacerdotalism. None whatever. The new covenant knows nothing of inherent grace in material things or actions. The new covenant knows nothing of a special priesthood. In fact, the biblical doctrine of the new covenant is categorical: it resolutely holds to the priesthood of *all* believers; every believer is a minister of the new covenant. This is not merely a slogan. It is a glorious fact.

Oh! The new covenant does, of course, know of a special priesthood, and it has a special priest. This priesthood has only one member, only one priest – the Lord Jesus Christ. In this sense, the new covenant is fully sacerdotal – *but only in this sense.*

Christ is a sacerdotal priest – in the full sense of the word:

Jesus... has a permanent priesthood. Therefore he is able to save completely those who come to God through him... Such a high priest meets our need – one who is holy, blameless, pure, set apart from sinners, exalted above the heavens. Unlike the other high priests, he does not need to offer sacrifices day after day, first for his own sins, and then for the sins of the people. He sacrificed for their sins once for all when he offered himself. For the law appoints as high priests men who are weak; but the oath, which came after the law, appointed the Son, who has been made perfect forever... Christ... as high priest... went through the greater and more perfect tabernacle that is not man-made, that is to say, not a part of this creation. He did not enter by means of the blood of goats and calves; but he entered the Most Holy Place once for all by his own blood, having obtained eternal redemption. The blood of goats and bulls and the ashes of a heifer sprinkled on those who are ceremonially unclean sanctify them so that they are outwardly clean. How much more, then, will the blood of Christ, who through the eternal Spirit offered himself unblemished to God, cleanse our consciences from acts that lead to death, so that we may serve the living God! For this reason Christ is the mediator of a new covenant, that those who are called may receive the promised eternal inheritance – now that he has died as a ransom to set them free from the sins committed under the first covenant... When this priest had offered for all time one sacrifice for sins, he sat down at the right hand of God. Since that time he waits for his enemies to be made his footstool, because by one sacrifice he has made perfect forever those who are being made holy (Heb. 7:24-28; 9:11 – 10:14).

Moreover, Christ is a sacerdotal intercessor – in the full sense of the word:

Who will bring any charge against those whom God has chosen? It is God who justifies. Who is he that condemns? Christ Jesus, who died – more than that, who was raised to life – is at the right hand of God and is also interceding for us (Rom. 8:33-34; see also Rom. 8:27).
Because Jesus lives forever... he is able to save completely those who come to God through him, because he always lives to intercede for them (Heb. 7:24-25).

And therein lies my point; *that* is why I am writing. Sacramentalism and sacerdotalism are more than appalling dangers for men; they fiendishly undermine the Lord Jesus Christ himself –

his sacerdotal person and his sacerdotal work. And, in the ultimate, this is what makes them abominable.

The Church of Rome, of course, is both sacramental and sacerdotal. Do not, however, run away with the idea that sacramentalism and sacerdotalism are confined to Romanists. Far from it! The magisterial Reformers[1] went badly astray at this point. Grievously clinging to the sacramental doctrine and practice they inherited from the Fathers and the medieval Church, time and again they had their backs to the wall, trying to fend off Roman taunts and challenges over the issue. Unsurprisingly, they were not always successful, since both sides were so strongly wedded to the Fathers and the medieval: Rome had too much to catch hold of where the Reformers were concerned, and scored too many hits for comfort.

The shadow cast by Reformed sacramentalism has been long and deep. In my *Infant Baptism Tested*, I fully documented the evidence, showing how sacramentalism has played havoc among the Reformed – starting with Calvin, through the time of the Puritans, the Westminster Assembly documents, right down to the present-day advocates of the Federal Vision.[2] And sacerdotalism is never far away from sacramentalism.

Moreover, all this applies far wider than the Reformed. Many evangelicals, dissenters, Nonconformists, Baptists... like their bit of sacerdotalism. Oh yes they do! As I showed in my *Baptist Sacramentalism*, in recent years the weeds of sacramentalism and

---

[1] 'Magisterial' because they, going to the old covenant for their system, thought the magistrate should enforce religion.

[2] 'Federal Vision', stemming from the Auburn Conference in Monroe in 2002, is the name of a group of Presbyterians who assert that the magisterial Reformers and the Westminster Confession, building on the Fathers, taught baptismal regeneration. As I showed in my *Infant*, they have plenty to get their teeth into. What is more, the advocates of the Federal Vision allege that those who claim to be heirs of the Reformers – Calvin in particular – and the Westminster documents, have in the main drifted away from this sacramental position. Starting from this premise, they consistently and overtly go the whole hog with sacramentalism, to the utter ruination of the biblical doctrine of conversion, with catastrophic results.

sacerdotalism have taken root in such unlikely fields. I am very sorry to say that they are showing signs of vigorous growth.[3] Since I last warned about the matter, the number of publications about and by the Fathers has proceeded unabated.[4] Again, although I will not expand on it here, I detect a growing return to Calvin's view of the Lord's supper – a development with which I am out of sympathy, to put it mildly.

Such is the background to this present work.

In this slim volume, I tackle an issue which, in its turn, makes its sorry contribution to the long-running saga of the unbiblical notions of sacramentalism and sacerdotalism; namely the use of the laying on of hands in ordination of ministers or pastors. I more than tackle it. This book represents my latest effort to stem the tide of sacramentalism, rolling, as it does, remorselessly towards sacerdotalism. I therefore make no apology for being overtly negative: sacramentalism and sacerdotalism are great evils in this day of the new covenant, spelling the eternal ruin of millions.

---

[3] Sacramentalism is far more widespread, and more deeply embedded than many allow. Take the Coronation ceremony in the UK. This is both heavily sacramental and sacerdotal. This should cause no surprise. Where did the authorities go when they wanted to set it up? They went to the old covenant! For more, see 'Religion & the Coronation' (27th May 2013) on bbciplayer. And then this: 'The Communion service proceeds. After the Creed the choir sings Veni, Creator Spiritus, the ancient hymn invoking the Holy Spirit, the Sovereign's crimson robe is removed and she is seated in the Coronation Chair (placed facing the altar). Four Knights of the Garter hold a canopy over the Chair and, concealed from view, the Archbishop anoints the Sovereign with holy oil on the hands, the breast and the head. This is the most solemn part of the coronation service, for by anointing the monarch is set apart or consecrated for the duties of a Sovereign. Meanwhile the choir sings the anthem Zadok the Priest, the words of which (from the first Book of Kings) have been sung at every coronation since King Edgar's in 973' ('Guide to the Coronation Service – Westminster Abbey', www.westminster-abbey.org). I leave the original capitals.

[4] As I write, an evangelical publishing house has brought out a series of books on 'famous' Christians, lumping together the Reformed, the evangelical and the patristic. I wonder how many are aware of the subtle – subliminal – implication this involves?

The creation of a privileged class of believers presents a danger to the priesthood of all believers and to the mediatorship of Christ... When the Spirit of God 'lays hands on' men and women at conversion, this is their consecration, their call to serve their high priest, Jesus Christ. They become members of the royal priesthood; they are the Levites of the new covenant. God has made provision for their ordination at [conversion]. They need no other

Marjorie Warkentin

Oh, that it could be said to the churches today: 'The house of Jacob shall possess their possessions'

David Gay, quoting Obadiah 17, NKJV

Introduction

Since many of today's evangelical and Reformed churches still practice the laying on of hands in ordination, and since – as I showed in my *The Pastor: Does He Exist?* – it has played a very significant part in the history of the corruption of Christ's system of church governance and care, we ought to examine the supposed biblical grounds for the practice.[1]

The burden of what I want to say is admirably caught in the apostle's word to the Colossians: 'I have been made a servant of the church by God' (Col. 1:25, GNB). Too often, however, this past 1800 years men have so-say been made a servant of God by the Church! And the change in word order is the least of the troubles! Within that change lies a practice that can only be called *diabolical*. And ordination is at the heart of it.

Down the centuries, the laying on of hands has made a huge contribution to the fostering of the great evil of sacramentalism. While, I admit, most of today's evangelical and Reformed churches have a (fairly) low view of ordination coupled with the laying on of hands, nevertheless, sacramentalism is never far removed from the procedure – even in those churches. As always, it is what people in the pew think – not what the theologians tell them to think; most people just do not follow the metaphysical arguments and escape-clauses which are used to bolster the practice, even if they bother to listen to them. For this reason, mysticism – not to say, mystification – leading to superstition and thence to sacramentalism, is an ever-present danger associated with the rite.

This is no ivory-tower study. As I have said, sacramentalism and a return to the Fathers is on the march these days – and in the most surprising of quarters. The laying on of hands, therefore, unless properly weighed in the balances according to Scripture, may yet mistakenly come to play a very important role in the churches in

---

[1] For my supporting arguments throughout this book, see both my *Pastor* and my *Priesthood*.

the not-too-distant future. It may yet assume its full sacramental – not to say, sacerdotal – dress, even in some of today's most 'orthodox' of evangelical or Reformed churches. May? If things go on as they are, I am pretty sure it will. Already, where the rite is used, it is regarded as the pinnacle of the ordination service. I am trying to get to grips, therefore, with something that is far from trivial.

Let me explain how I intend to go about it. First, I will briefly summarise the history and development of the rite, starting with the Fathers. Then I will look at Scripture – that is, the relevant New Testament passages which are used by advocates of the practice – to show that this history cannot be justified biblically. I am not doing it this way round, I hasten to add, because I think history carries more weight than Scripture. Not at all. But were it not for the tragic history of this practice, starting with the appalling changes brought in by the Fathers, and all the consequences entailed in that, I would never have had to write. So that is why I begin with the history. It makes grim reading.

As you come to [Christ]... you... like living stones, are being built into a spiritual house to be a holy priesthood, offering spiritual sacrifices acceptable to God through Jesus Christ... You are a chosen people, a royal priesthood, a holy nation, a people belonging to God, that you may declare the praises of him who called you out of darkness into his wonderful light. Once you were not a people, but now you are the people of God; once you had not received mercy, but now you have received mercy

1 Peter 2:4-10

Sadly, 'our forefathers went down into Egypt, and we lived there many years'

David Gay, quoting Numbers 20:15

The History of the Rite

To discover the history of the laying on of hands in ordination, we have to go outside Scripture. And, as with so many errors in doctrine and practice introduced into the church, we have to start with the Fathers.

A glance at the history of the rite in the time of the Fathers

The laying on of hands in ordination to church office was invented by the Fathers. But, as Marjorie Warkentin noted, at the beginning the laying on of hands was not connected to ordination. The Fathers originally confined the rite of the laying on of hands to baptism. I make no comment at this stage; I simply record the fact:

Archaeological finds in Rome (3rd century) illustrate baptism as accompanied by the laying on of hands, with the dove (representing the Holy Spirit) about to descend on the young baptismal candidate. Cyprian and his fellow-bishops, meeting in council in 256, decided that the proper outward sign of the bestowal of the Spirit was the imposition of hands. The baptism of infants led to the need for confirmatory rites such as anointing with oil, and making the sign of the cross on the forehead of the candidate, and then to the later rite of confirmation. Whichever rite or aspect of a rite received the emphasis, some of the Fathers considered human agency essential to the reception of the Spirit, the human agent being the priest. Basil of Caesarea, writing in the 4th century, justifies these practices on the basis of secret traditions, traditions reserved for the hierarchy, and hidden from the eyes of 'inquisitive meddlers'.

Not all the Fathers agreed with all this – Athanasius, Cyril of Jerusalem, Hilary, Chrysostom among them. Nevertheless, as infant baptism tightened its grip:

Confirmation assumed greater importance. In the laying on of hands, the bishop conferred the Spirit through his special apostolic powers received at his [own] ordination. According to Cyprian (3rd century), this authority was derived not only through succession, but because every bishop is inducted into his office by God's special decree, and received special revelations of the Spirit. Since only the bishop could confirm, and only the confirmed could partake of the Eucharist, the central rite of the Church, the bishops quickly gained control over the lives of the faithful, for to rebel against the bishop was to rebel against God... Social, political and religious pressures contributed to the growth of an impregnable religious hierarchy. The imposition of hands was a visible reminder of the unassailable authority of the prelacy. In the coming struggles with the so-called heretics and the secular princes, those who could claim custody of the power of God had an invaluable asset.[1]

That is, the Church authorities claimed that they alone had God's truth and God's authority, thus dismissing – and damning – at a stroke, all dissension and all dissenters. Thus it ever was; thus it ever is.[2]

Warkentin then traced out the way in which this notion – the new-found reality – of the power of the priests extended from baptism to ordination to the ministry:

The sacred was the sphere of the clergy; the secular that of the laity. Christianity became identified with an institution and its cultic[3] observances; 'Church' had become an organisation. Liturgy and theology became the province of bishops and priests; the world of work and war belonged to the laity – not as autonomous agents, but as a potent force to be used by the clergy in the power struggles with the political rulers. The practice of infant baptism had done much to rob the community of the new covenant of its distinctive character as a people set apart, a royal priesthood to serve God in all aspects of life, cultic and cultural. As the gateway to the sacerdotal realm, it was inevitable that ordination should become the keystone of the hierarchical structure... 'Ordination is the basis of all other powers'.[4] So it became in the early centuries of the Church...
When Constantine proclaimed Christianity as the religion of the State, Church leadership patterns were buttressed by political sanction. Heresy consisted in anything that threatened this... The forms of the

---

[1] Warkentin pp32-33.
[2] I recall, when I was a very young man, suggesting to 'a leading brother', the virtual pope of the assembly, consideration of some change – the introduction of some stated preaching – and getting his sharp and immediate response: 'We have all the truth'! I will return to this point.
[3] That is, belonging to a religious system, ceremonial, ritual.
[4] Warkentin was quoting Piet Fransen, giving the Catholic view.

Old Testament sacrificial system, combined with elements of [Greek] hierarchicalism were now thoroughly entrenched: the Church was secure at last... Reliance on Old Testament paradigms shaped organisational forms... In the writings of the Fathers, the priests, Levites, elders and prophets became the models for the ministry... Ordination set the clergy up and apart from the people of God... Only the ordained... could baptise, confirm and ordain. Only they, through the power they had received when hands were laid on them, were able to re-enact the sacrifice of Christ in the Mass. The ordinary believer, generally illiterate and ignorant, was at the mercy of the educated clergy... The ordination rite was strengthened by pageantry and symbolic accoutrements, but the actual transmission of spiritual power occurred when the bishop laid his hands on the head of the kneeling candidate. This was the climax of the whole ordination ceremony.[5]

And then we have Philip Schaff:

The ordination of clergymen was as early as the 4th or 5th century admitted into the number of sacraments. Augustine [354-430] first calls it a sacrament, but with the remark that in his time the Church unanimously acknowledged the sacramental character of this usage. Ordination is the solemn consecration to the special priesthood...[6] It is [claimed to be] the medium of communicating the gifts for the ministerial office. It confers the capacity and authority of administering the sacraments and governing the body of believers, and secures to the Church, order, care and steady growth to the end of time... Ordination was performed by the laying on of hands and prayer, closing with communion... Only bishops can ordain, though presbyters assist.[7]

Or so it was thought! Such ideas may have seemed small at the start, but as so often before and since, little events cast long and ever-darkening shadows. Whether or not we like to admit it, whether or not we know it, here – in novelties invented in the 4th and 5th centuries – we unearth the root of today's commonplace

---

[5] Warkentin pp40,41,45-51,103-105.
[6] I remind you, reader, in the new covenant it is the priesthood of all believers. Under the Fathers, the Church was taken back to the old covenant, and had a special priesthood – a priesthood of the few – foisted upon it.
[7] Schaff pp489-491.

approach to ordination to 'the pastorate' in Reformed and evangelical circles.

How did the Reformation affect the rite?

What did the Reformers do with what they inherited as the legacy of the medieval Church in this regard? As the principal theologian of the Reformation, John Calvin's role is pivotal. And we know that Calvin held to both ordination and the laying on of hands:

As the matter of introducing [the minister], it is good to use the [laying on] of hands, which ceremony was observed by the apostles [Calvin was begging the question] and then in the ancient Church [that is, the Fathers], providing that it takes place without superstition and without offence.

I pause. Some hope! Calvin thought so too: 'But because there has been much superstition in the past and scandal might result, it is better to abstain from it because of the infirmity of the times'.[8]

Even so, commenting on Acts 14:23, Calvin declared:

The Greek word, *cheirotonein*, signifies to decree, or ordain a thing, by lifting up the hands, as they used to do in the assemblies of the people. [In other words, by voting]. Notwithstanding, ecclesiastical writers often use the word *cheirotoneia* in another sense; to wit, for their solemn rite of ordaining, which is called in Scripture, 'laying on of hands'. Furthermore, by this manner of speech is very excellently expressed the right way to ordain pastors. Paul and Barnabas are said to choose [to elect] elders. Do they this alone by their private office? No, but rather they allow the matter to be decided by the consent of them [that is, believers] all. Therefore, in ordaining pastors, the people had their free election, but lest there should any tumult arise, Paul and Barnabas sit as chief moderators. Thus must the decree of the Council of Laodicea be understood, which forbids that the people have a liberty granted them to elect.[9]

So what was Calvin's settled position? We know that he wanted us to take his definitive view of everything – including the laying on of hands – from his *Institutes*. He told us so. First in general:

---

[8] Warkentin p60, quoting Calvin: *Ecclesiastical Ordinances*.
[9] Calvin: *Commentaries* Vol.19 Part 1 pp27-28. See below for my comments on this.

I have endeavoured [here in the *Institutes*] to give such a summary of religion in all its parts... Having thus... paved the way, I shall not feel it necessary, in any Commentaries on Scripture which I may afterwards publish, to enter into long discussions of doctrine... In this way, the pious reader will be saved much trouble and weariness, provided he comes furnished with a knowledge of the [*Institutes*] as an essential prerequisite... seeing that I have in a manner deduced at length all the articles which pertain to Christianity.[10]

And then in particular:

It was the custom and ordinary practice of the apostles to ordain ministers by the laying on of hands. As to this ceremony, and its origin and meaning, I have formerly given a brief explanation of them, and the rest may be learned from the *Institutes*.[11]

Very well. Let's have a look at the *Institutes*. Calvin:

It is certain that when the apostles appointed anyone to the ministry, they used no other ceremony than the laying on of hands... It was the regular form, whenever they called anyone to the sacred ministry. In this way they consecrated pastors and teachers... Though there is no fixed precept concerning the laying on of hands, yet as we see that it was uniformly observed by the apostles... It is certainly useful that by such a symbol the dignity of the ministry should be commended to the people, and he who is ordained, reminded that he is no longer his own, but bound in service to God and the Church. Besides, it will not prove an empty sign, if it is restored to its genuine origin... provided it be not superstitiously abused.[12]

Hmm! Since Calvin was unequivocal, saying: 'It is certain that when the apostles appointed anyone to the ministry, they used no other ceremony than the laying on of hands', and since I cannot put the question to Calvin himself, may I ask those who agree with Calvin: How many men did the apostles appoint to 'the ministry'? Could we be given the name of *one*? If so, would someone give us his name? And what proof is there that the apostles laid hands on

---

[10] Calvin: *Institutes* Vol.1 pp21,23, in his prefixed explanations for the work dated 1539 and 1545.
[11] Calvin: *Commentaries* Vol.21 Part 3 pp116-117.
[12] Calvin: *Institutes* Vol.2 p326.

such men – if they existed? I can see no scripture to justify Calvin's categorical assertions.[13]

Besides, Calvin was trying to run with hare and hounds. When the men and women in the pew are taught, according to Calvin's dictum, that ordination appoints a man to the ministry, and that the laying on of hands is not an empty sign, and that one of the aims in doing it is to impress the pew-holders with the dignity of the ministry, it doesn't take much imagination to see what those pew-holders might come to think about ordination and the laying on of hands, or what they might come to think of 'the ministry' and 'the minister'. Such a man must be the Lord's anointed! What else can he be? He must have *the* gift. He has been ordained, anointed. Do not touch the Lord's anointed! That's the 'hare'. As for the 'hounds', Calvin might drop in the caveat about superstition, but people don't read the small print! *Nor do ministers!*

Later, in his *Institutes*, in an extended section against the five additional Roman 'sacraments',[14] Calvin had a considerable amount to say about the laying on of hands. Speaking of the confirmation (another unbiblical invention!) of repentant heretics, and their confirmation by means of the laying on of hands, although Calvin thought Jerome laboured under a 'delusion when he says that the observance is apostolical', he nevertheless liked the way, as he put it, Jerome 'softens the expression when he adds, that this benediction is given to bishops only, more in honour of the priesthood than from any necessity of law. This laying on of hands, which is done simply by way of benediction, I commend, and would like to see restored to its pure use in the present day'.

As for the apostolic practice in Acts 8:15-17, Calvin was clear:

Did this ministry, which the apostles then performed, still remain in the Church, it would also behove us to observe the laying on of hands: but since that gift has ceased to be conferred, to what end is the laying on of hands? Assuredly the Holy Spirit is still present with the people of God; without his guidance and direction the Church of God cannot subsist. For we have a promise of perpetual duration, by which Christ invites the thirsty to come to him, that they may drink living water (John 7:37). But those miraculous powers and manifest operations,

---

[13] I will look at 1 Tim. 4:14.
[14] Calvin: *Institutes* Vol.2 pp622-649.

which were distributed by the laying on of hands, have ceased. They were only for a time.

On the other hand: 'The laying on of hands... I admit it to be a sacrament in true and legitimate ordination'.[15]

I know I am jumping ahead, but, we ought to take note of Calvin on 2 Timothy 1:6, when he was expanding his comments to come to the general:

Paul... here speaks of ordination; that is, of the solemn act of conferring [note the word] the office of the ministry... I think... that Paul here speaks of the office of a pastor.

I pause. Calvin has embarked on 'assumption' here, reading back into the text the post-apostolic notion of both 'ordination' and 'the office of the ministry', 'the pastor'. As for the former, he read back into the New Testament the so-called power of the rite; as for the latter, he read back into the New Testament the very existence of the office. Putting it more simply: both rite and office were unknown in the New Testament. Having gone as far as he did, however, Calvin then generalised his claims beyond all warrant!

Nevertheless, let him go on:

That point being settled[!], it is asked: 'Was grace given by the outward sign?' To this question I answer, whenever ministers were ordained... grace from God was obtained for them by prayer, and was not given to them by virtue of the sign, although the sign was not uselessly and unprofitably employed, but was a sure pledge of that grace which they received from God's own hand. That ceremony was not a profane act, invented for the sole purpose of procuring credit in the eyes of men, but a lawful consecration before God, which is not performed but by the power of the Holy Spirit. Besides, Paul takes the sign for the whole matter or the whole transaction; for he declares that Timothy was endued with grace, when he was offered to God [*sic*] as a minister... Paul ordained [Timothy] to the ministry.[16]

Phew! See my earlier comments on hares and hounds. I have pointed out this kind of double-speak in Calvin on countless

---

[15] See my *Pastor* for extracts. While Calvin was against the miraculous, he was for the laying on of hands.
[16] Calvin: *Commentaries* Vol.21 Part 3 pp189-190.

occasions.[17] If Calvin were alive, I would respectfully ask him to get off the fence, once and for all. Was he a sacramentalist or not? In previous works, I have shown that he held to the baptism of infants sacramentally. Now we can see his sacramentalism in ordination – grace is given by the rite, and the man is offered to God, consecrated. No wonder many of Calvin's consistent followers are sacramentalists, and have cogently argued that the Westminster documents are decidedly so.

All this is not only wrong; it is highly dangerous. I remind you, reader, not to forget that sacerdotalism is the next stop after sacramentalism.

Calvin, of course, was not alone in this way of going on. In short, as Warkentin stated:

Ordination with the laying on of hands survived the Reformation, but in the process lost both form and content. Romish embellishments were removed; content was re-formed in keeping with the theological positions of the various groups, and their need to preserve their organisational integrity. Six facts stand out:

1. Ordination with prayer and the imposition of hands continued to be the norm in the induction of church officers. Even those who discontinued the rite tended later to restore it to use.

2. Although in Protestantism ordination was not one of the 'seven sacraments of the Church', it did retain a sacramental or semi-sacramental character in some denominations (notably the Anglican). Even among Baptists, a sacramental understanding of the act of the laying on of hands tended to re-assert itself in times of stress.

3. In the rejection of sacramentalism, the rite became representative...

4. Even among those who denied a person-to-person apostolic succession from Peter, the idea of succession through personal agency persisted...

5. Ordination was an integral part of the doctrine of the ministry. Changes in the function of the 'minister' brought changes to the doctrine and practice of ordination... Ordination now set apart the preacher instead of the priest. Since the imposition of hands continued to be the highlight of the ceremony, many of the ideas formerly associated with ordination under the old regime were carried over into

---

[17] See my *Infant*; *Baptist Sacramentalism*; *Pastor*.

Protestantism. Especially persistent were the idea of 'character' and succession. Ordination was still also the *sine qua non* for the administration of baptism and the Lord's supper.

6. ...Among Baptists there was overlap and selectivity in the use of proof-texts to support the laying on of hands in baptism and ordination. A study of the Baptist Confessions suggests that ordination practices were based not so much on Scripture as that Scripture was employed to justify practices that were deemed necessary to preserve denominational identity.

As a result of the Reformation, ordination with the laying on of hands lost authority. There were both theological and historical reasons for this. The decline in the sacramental understanding of the rite, and the altered view of the nature of apostolic succession, led to a shift in the basis on which the authority of the clergy rested. A sense of special 'call' over and above the general call of all believers to ministry, a sort of ecclesiastical 'divine right', became the chief argument for right to church office. Historically, it had became apparent that whether or not ordination had preceded the preaching of the word made no difference to its effectiveness. Whatever ordination might do for church structure, the gospel could be preached successfully without it.[18]

Nevertheless, the damage had been done. The seed having been sown, the harvest was inevitable.

But John Gill was rightly adamant. There is no scriptural warrant for the practice. Commenting on Acts 14:23, he declared:

Though there was 'a stretching out of the hands', yet there was no 'imposition of hands' used at the ordination – neither of extraordinary officers, as apostles, nor of ordinary pastors or elders of churches, in the times of Christ and his apostles. Christ ordained the twelve apostles himself, but we read not a word of his laying his hands upon them when he ordained them; nor of the seventy... Matthias (Acts 1:22-26)... no mention is made of any hands being laid on him... The apostles are said to ordain elders in every church, not by laying their hands upon them, [but] when they declared the elders duly elected and ordained, as before observed. The apostle directed Titus (Tit. 1:5)... to ordain elders in every city... but gave him no orders and instructions to lay hands upon them; which he would not have omitted had it been material, and so essential to ordination as some make it to be...

No [scriptural] instance can be given of hands being laid on any ordinary minister, pastor or elder, at his ordination; nor, indeed, of

---

[18] Warkentin pp84-86; see also pp103-105.

hands being laid on any, upon whatsoever account, but by extraordinary persons; nor by them upon any ministers, but extraordinary ones; and even then not at and for the ordination of them... Acts 13:1-3 is no proof of laying on of hands at the ordination of a pastor or elder of a church...

Paul, indeed, speaks of the hands of the presbytery being laid upon Timothy (1 Tim. 4:14), but it should be observed that Timothy was an extraordinary officer in the church, an evangelist [but *not* in the sense the word is used today – DG], and was not chosen or ordained a pastor of any particular church... Upon the whole, it appears to be an extraordinary affair transacted by extraordinary occasions on an extraordinary [person], and by it an extraordinary gift was conveyed; which no man of modesty will assume to himself a power of conveying. The hands of ministers now being empty, and they having no gifts to convey through the use of this rite, of course it ought to cease, and should, it not appearing to have been used but by extraordinary persons on any account, upon which, at least for the most part, extraordinary things follow. To say that this rite is now used at the ordination of a pastor to point him out to the assembly, is exceeding trifling. The church needs it not, having before chosen and called him, and he having accepted their call in a more private way. And it is needless to others met together publicly to observe the order of the procedure... To use the rite to point him out to the people is such a piece of weakness for which no excuse can be made.[19]

Disregarding Gill's unfortunate ministerial language, he surely hit the nail on the head. Warkentin claimed that Gill saw 'that the laying on of hands could not be divorced from sacramental modes of thought'.[20] He was right!

So much for this thumbnail sketch of the history of the laying on of hands in ordination.

It is time to look at Scripture.

---

[19] Gill: *Body* pp246-250.
[20] Warkentin p84.

Paul, an apostle of Christ Jesus by the will of God... to the church of God in Corinth, together with all the saints throughout Achaia... Not that we are competent in ourselves to claim anything for ourselves, but our competence comes from God. He has made us competent as ministers of a new covenant

2 Corinthians 1:1; 3:5-6

Go and inquire of the LORD for me and for the remnant in Israel and Judah about what is written in this book that has been found. Great is the LORD's anger that is poured out on us because our fathers have not kept the word of the LORD; they have not acted in accordance with all that is written in this book

2 Chronicles 34:21

The Scriptures Examined

Leaving aside the history of the rite, the question is: Does Scripture warrant the laying on of hands in ordination? There are eight passages which the advocates of ordination by the laying on of hands use to try to justify their practice; namely, Acts 6:6; 8:14-19; 9:1-19; 13:3; 19:6; 1 Timothy 4:14; 5:22; 2 Timothy 1:6. Let us look at them all.

Before we begin, let me make one thing clear. I am not trying to set out a consistent and categorical scheme of interpretation of these texts, one which commands universal support. No one has yet managed *that*. I certainly have no illusions about it, nor do I attempt it. My purpose is much more limited, and avowedly negative – to show that from these scriptures no case can be made for ordination to the so-called pastoral office by means of the rite of the laying on of hands. Although I admit the limited nature of this objective, I do not concede that 'limited' means 'insignificant'!

Another point: the fact that no one can give us a scheme that is consistent with the New Testament, and that after 2000 years, surely ought to raise a red flag right at the start.

Before I come to the eight texts I have listed, what about Hebrews 6:2? Why have I not included it in my list? Before I respond to that, let me quote the passage in question:

Therefore let us leave the elementary teachings about Christ, and go on to maturity, not laying again the foundation of repentance from acts that lead to death [useless rituals, footnote], and of faith in God, instruction about baptisms, the laying on of hands, the resurrection of the dead, and eternal judgement. And, God permitting, we will do so (Heb. 6:1-3).

Well, whatever else this passage teaches, it certainly has nothing to say about the laying on of hands in connection with ordination. Nothing at all! Ordination is not in the passage. Nor is it anywhere close in the context.

In brief, I suggest that Hebrews 6:1-3 is all of a piece with the rest of the letter to the Hebrews, in which the writer, deeply anxious to keep believers from going back to the old covenant, refers to various shadowy practices and doctrines of that covenant – the sacrificial system, the levitical priesthood, the apparatus of old-covenant worship, and so on. He takes those practices and institutions, one by one, and with invincible clarity proves that Christ has fulfilled, and therefore abolished, them all (Heb. 7:11-28; 8:6-13; 10:15-18). Not only that. He shows that in every instance, Christ is 'better' – the keyword in the letter, appearing as it does some thirteen times on my reckoning. In particular, in this passage the writer has in mind Jewish washings and *their* laying on of hands. 'Don't go back to the old covenant', is his constant cry. And that is what he is doing here. Such is my suggested interpretation of the passage.

For those who don't like my suggestion, before they reject it outright they ought to face the detailed arguments in the works of Arthur W.Pink and Marjorie Warkentin.[1] I acknowledge that one of my favourite commentators, John Brown, disagrees with me.[2] Nor can I cite John Calvin or John Owen in support. Nevertheless, I still (fairly confidently) hold my ground. I am one with Pink:

> The interpretation which I shall give... is not at all in accord with that advanced by... Calvin, Owen and Gouge... J.Brown. Much as I respect their works, and deeply as I am indebted to not a little that is helpful in them, yet I dare not follow them blindly.[3]

In any case, as I say, whatever is meant by 'the laying on of hands' in Hebrews 6:1-3, it has nothing to do with ordination to church office. That is why I left the passage off my list. So let's get on.

Laying on of hands in Acts

An interesting, though seemingly small, point: I notice that the NIV often talks of 'placing hands',[4] whereas the AV, NKJV and

---

[1] Pink pp272-284; Warkentin pp115-119.

[2] Brown: *Hebrews* p275.

[3] Pink p272. I have changed Pink's affectation, 'we', to what he really meant; namely, 'I'.

[4] As do the GNB and NEB. The NIV and GNB both drop back into 'laying' in 1 and 2 Timothy. I wonder why.

NASB use 'laying on of hands'. It has crossed my mind that the NIV has rightly kicked a hole in this bit of ecclesiastical jargon, and, in so doing, has rendered us all an excellent service.[5] As I say, we are looking at Acts 6:6; 8:14-19; 9:1-19; 13:3; 19:6. All these, at one time or another, have been dragooned into use to support the laying on of hands in ordination. I use 'dragooned' deliberately. No matter what the scholars, theologians, commentators, teachers and preachers may say about these five passages, they agree on at least one thing – *they, the teachers, disagree with each other!* More than that, they are highly selective as to which passages they apply to ordination, and which passages they do not. In fact, the unifying factor in all their interpretations seems to be that it is impossible to fit these texts into a consistent scheme. And this is precisely the point I made when dealing with the sacramentalists' attempt to fit the Acts passages on baptism into a unified sacramental scheme. As I said in my *Baptist Sacramentalism* (having already spoken similarly in my *Infant Baptism Tested*):

Not every detail in Acts (or the Gospels) should be taken as normative for church practice; the letters are designed for that purpose. Acts records a transition period, a time of explosive spiritual power when extraordinary things were going on – some unique in the history of the church. And I mean unique, never (whatever some may claim) to be repeated. That being the case, just as hard cases make bad law, so to use extraordinary – unique – events as normative for the church today, is far from sensible... Acts reads very differently. Far from being a 'normal' history, some events are given much space, while several months or even years are telescoped into a few words, according to their importance in Luke's overall scheme. Note, perhaps in particular, the way the history tails off with Paul in Rome. Luke, it is clear, did not intend to give a sedate history, a measured account, rounded and nicely balanced – as editors and publishers would demand today. Rather, recording volcanic events, he did not concern himself with the precise order within each eruption, nor did he stand back and formulate a theology for church practice, but left that for others.[6]

---

[5] Similarly, to use 'speak in languages' is better than 'speak in tongues'.

[6] Gay: *Infant* pp17,33; *Baptist Sacramentalism* pp195,197,304.

Getting back to the issue in hand, no simple, clear ordination-scheme has yet (in 2000 years!) been enunciated which comfortably encompasses all the passages in Acts. And until someone comes up with such a scheme, I think we may be allowed to treat with caution any extravagant claim, based on Acts, for the laying on of hands in connection with ordination. Indeed, we *ought* to treat such a claim with caution.

The following points should be borne in mind. Luke was very much aware that the events he was recording, both in his Gospel and in the Acts, were a direct fulfilment of God's Old Testament promises of the new covenant, and he saw this in terms of the working of God's 'hand', *cheir*. Take Acts 4:28. The Jews and Gentiles crucified Christ. The believers, addressing God, spoke of it in this way: 'They did what your power [hand, AV, NKJV, NASB] (*cheir*) and will had decided beforehand should happen'. In other words, God's hand, God's will, God's power, are one and the same. This is how the early believers saw it. This use of 'hand', therefore, is a metaphor for the powerful working out of God's will and power in the affairs of men.[7] Luke was very fond of the figure. See Luke 1:1,66; 7:48; 17:24; 20:19; 21:12; 22:21,25; 24:50; Acts 7:25,35,48; 9:8; 11:21; 13:11; 14:23; 17:24; 22:11,14; 27:19, for instance.[8]

So what can we deduce from this? Warkentin:

Those texts in which Luke speaks of the laying on of hands must be interpreted in the context of his penchant for using 'hand' to express the will or plan of God as he moves among his people to establish his kingdom (Acts 1:6). To isolate these texts from each other or from their function in the whole of Luke-Acts is to invite distortion of their meaning. For Luke, the events he narrates in the interval during which

---

[7] I admit that there is one striking exception to this; namely, Pentecost. I am unable to account for it. I simply record the fact. It is true to say, however, that Peter quotes Joel, and repeats the words himself, to declare that God had 'poured out' the Spirit to produce the amazing works so evident that day (Acts 2:17,33). Whether or not we should read 'hand' into this act of pouring, I leave to your judgement, reader. I am happy to do so myself. Since God is speaking to us as a man, how else can a man 'pour out' but by using his hand to lift and tilt the vessel?

[8] Some of these are more evident in the Greek. See Warkentin p123.

the Spirit carries on the ministry of Jesus are events ordained by the hand of God. Just as God gave the tribes of Canaan into the 'hands' of the Israelites (see Josh. 2:24; 4:24; 6:2; 8:1,7; 10:8,19,30,32; *etc.*), he will now do the same for the new Israel. The laying-on-of-hands episodes occur as milestones[9] in the fulfilment theme of Luke, events foreordained by God and fulfilled by the Spirit of Jesus...
Luke... uses [laying on of hands] as a hermeneutical [explanatory] tool in interpreting the fulfilment of promise in the new Israel. Because this motif includes the term 'hand', representing the will and plan of God, it is eminently suitable for this purpose.

To ignore this overall purpose in the spiritually explosive time of the apostles, is to leave us exposed to the nonsense of trying to force the individual texts into a settled consistent pattern or norm for us today – which can only lead to impossible outcomes. The fact is, the epoch-marking events of those early days defy a simple, consistent explanation. Indeed, Luke never recorded them for us as normative. They are anything but. Warkentin again: 'It becomes apparent before long that attempts to construct doctrinal formulas from these [Acts] texts result in bewildering contradictions'. Having raised several questions illustrating these 'contradictions' in the vain efforts men have made to formulate a consistent interpretation embracing all the texts,[10] she went on:

We might pose other questions, but we have already demonstrated the theological diversity of these texts. Could it be that we are asking the *wrong* questions? The grammatical ambiguities we encounter might suggest as much.[11]

As I said in my aforementioned books, while I understand Warkentin's (and others') use of 'milestones' – that Luke was noting 'milestones' along the way as the gospel advanced throughout the world – the word is too placid, conjuring up, as it does, the present day church (at least for many of us in the UK), plodding on its weary way. Acts reads very differently. Luke's

---

[9] See immediately below.
[10] Questions such as: Was the laying on of hands apostolic only? Do the texts explicitly state that a gift was a gift conveyed by the rite? Was the rite performed **because** *the candidates were qualified*, or *to* **make** *them qualified?* Did the rite lead to church office?
[11] Warkentin pp123-124,126-127, emphasis hers.

history could be more aptly described, as I have said, as 'volcanic'. He talks in terms of eruptions or dramatic interventions; certainly not milestones.

The point is, however, there is no settled normative pattern here. This is not a criticism. Luke never intended to set out such a pattern. That was not his purpose at all. He was recording spiritual explosions. And these volcanic explosions do not represent the settled pattern of church life.

So much for the overall view of the Acts passages. It is now time to look at them individually. But we must not forget this vital introduction. There is no overall scheme or pattern that I can discern – or, within my experience, that anybody else has yet discovered.

The Greeks in Jerusalem (Acts 6:1-7)

At the opening of Acts 6, the number of converts in the church at Jerusalem had swelled to such an extent that it led to a problem over the distribution of food to needy believers, one which, sad to say, involved a measure of racial tension. The apostles rightly saw to it that the matter was sorted out. Nevertheless, refusing themselves to be diverted from their spiritual work, they instructed the believers to choose seven suitable men to deal with the problem. The believers duly elected seven men whom 'they presented... to the apostles, who prayed and laid their hands on them'.

Several points must be noted. There is no suggestion of ordination of the seven to any office. None whatsoever. The work in question might well have been no more than a one-off responsibility to sort out a temporary problem; indeed, it has all the appearance of being such. As for the notion that the seven men were church officers on a permanent basis, we do not know that they even stayed in Jerusalem! Philip certainly didn't. So he could not possibly have continued to supervise the dining arrangements on a day-to-day basis. After all, when the Jerusalem church was scattered (Acts 8:1), we read that he was itinerant, went to Samaria, the desert road to Gaza, and to Azotus and Caesarea (Acts 8:5,26,40). As for Stephen, there is no suggestion that anybody replaced him after he was killed by stoning (Acts 7).

So the authority for the common view – that the seven who had hands laid on them were deacons, permanent church officers – is not to be found in the New Testament. Oh, there is authority for it, certainly – in Irenaeus![12] But not Scripture. I am not saying that we should not use the passage to deduce lessons for the qualifications and the work of the deacon, but I am saying that no one can be certain that the seven men were deacons. And to go on to use the passage to justify the ordination of 'pastors' or 'ministers' by the laying on of hands is a leap of wild proportions, a leap for which there is no warrant in this passage.

As a result, I do not see how this episode can safely be used to support ministerial ordination by the laying on of hands. It has nothing to do with the subject.

Gill spoke of the laying on of hands in this case as being done:

By extraordinary persons, the apostles, and it may be for extraordinary service, and so [be] no rule to ordinary ministers in the ordination of persons to an ordinary office... The use of it seems to be temporary, since we have no other instance of it on such account, nor any injunction of it, nor any direction for it, nor is it made mention of by the apostle, when he treats of the office of deacons, their qualifications, the proving, and instalment of them into their office, and their use of it (1 Tim. 3:10). Nor does it appear that there was afterwards any ordination of deacons, by imposition of hands, until the 4th century, when church-offices and church-officers were both magnified and multiplied. Besides, if the seven persons spoken of in Acts 6 were extraordinarily and *pro tempore* appointed to take care of the poor and of the widows in the first church at Jerusalem, and particularly of the Grecian widows in it, to answer their present [need, then they] were different from the ordinary deacons of the churches, afterwards spoken of in Paul's letters.

Gill, having given several reasons to support this suggestion, went on:

Nor does it appear that they continued in their office, but when this [need] was over, it ceased, and some of them, at least, were afterwards employed in other ministerial activities, and elsewhere – now if this was the case, which is not easy to be disproved, we have no scripture-

---

[12] Chadwick p48.

37

instance of the imposition of hands as the ordination of ordinary deacons nor any instruction and direction for it.[13]

Once again, allowing for Gill's use of 'ministerial' terminology, I think he got it right. At least, to use his own words, his view will take some disproving.

The Samaritans and the Ephesians (Acts 8:14-19 and 19:1-7)

Let me quote the relevant words from these passages:

> When the apostles... heard that Samaria had accepted the word of God, they sent Peter and John to them. When they arrived, they prayed for them that they might receive the Holy Spirit, because the Holy Spirit had not yet come upon any of them; they had simply been baptised into [in, footnote] the name of the Lord Jesus. Then Peter and John placed their hands on them, and they received the Holy Spirit. When Simon saw that the Spirit was given at the laying on of the apostles' hands... (Acts 8:14-19).

And:

> Paul... arrived at Ephesus. There he found some disciples and asked them: 'Did you receive the Holy Spirit when [after, footnote] you believed?' They answered: 'No, we have not even heard that there is a Holy Spirit'. So Paul asked: 'Then what baptism did you receive?' 'John's baptism', they replied... They were baptised into [in, footnote] the name of the Lord Jesus. When Paul placed his hands on them, the Holy Spirit came on them, and they spoke in other languages and prophesied... (Acts 19:1-7).

I think we may all agree; these two passages are unusual, difficult to expound, and virtually impossible to fit into any neat and simple scheme of interpretation; 'extraordinary' must be the word. Note also, it was apostles who laid their hands on others – whether Samaritans or Ephesians; extraordinary, yet again.

So, whatever the passages speak of, they do not give the slightest warrant for ordaining a man to office by means of laying on of hands. Nobody in either incident was ordained 'a pastor' or 'a minister'. Both events represent milestones – or, to use my terminology, volcanic eruptions – in the advance of the gospel in accordance with Christ's promise in Acts 1:8. In Acts 8, for

---

[13] Gill: *Body* pp250-251.

example, we have the record of how, to use Warkentin's happy expression, 'Pentecost has come to Samaria'. She concluded:

Luke clearly sees these new advances – to the Samaritans and to the Ephesians – as fulfilment of the promise of Acts 1:8. He uses Old Testament allusions and the Old Testament motif for the laying on of hands to show the significance of the arrival of the witness at Samaria and Ephesus.[14]

I agree. And whatever else may be argued from these two passages, I do not see how anyone can rightly use them to justify ordination to church office by laying on of hands. They have nothing to say on the subject.

Paul's conversion (Acts 9:1-19; 22:3-16; 26:9-18)
Here are the relevant sections of the passages. In all those passages, the laying on of hands is mentioned only in Acts 9:

The Lord told [Ananias]: 'Go to... Saul... In a vision he has seen a man named Ananias come and place his hands on him to restore his sight'... Ananias went to the house and entered it. Placing his hands on Saul, he said: 'Brother Saul, the Lord – Jesus, who appeared to you on the road... has sent me that you may see again and be filled with the Holy Spirit' (Acts 9:11-17).

Ananias laid hands on Saul, yes, but who can tell whether or not he did it in connection with Saul's being healed, his baptism, his reception of the Spirit, his commission to his life's work, or any combination of all four? From Christ's words to Ananias – namely, that Saul had seen, in a vision, 'Ananias come and place his hands on him to restore his sight' – it would be hard to argue against the claim that Ananias laid his hands on Saul for healing. As for Paul's office as an apostle, he himself was always adamant that his apostleship was by God's will and not of, through, or by any human agency (2 Cor. 1:1; 10.8; 13:10; Gal. 1:1,11-24; *etc.*).

What is more, bearing in mind not only what I have already said about Luke's description of events, but what I can only call his likening of the times of the Acts to the days of Moses for Israel, old-covenant overtones can be clearly seen in Luke's three accounts of the episode.

---

[14] Warkentin pp131-132.

Let me explain what I mean by this 'Moses connection'. Take Luke's recording of Christ's phrase, 'chosen instrument' – in Paul 'is my chosen instrument to carry my name before the Gentiles and their kings and before the people of Israel' (Acts 9:15). On hearing such words, can we not detect echoes of the launch of the old covenant? Let me remind you of the events just before the exodus:

The Israelites groaned in their slavery and cried out, and their cry for help because of their slavery went up to God. God heard their groaning and he remembered his covenant with Abraham, with Isaac and with Jacob. So God looked on the Israelites and was concerned about them (Ex. 2:23-25).

In his compassion, the LORD, therefore, appeared to Moses and commissioned him to deliver his people from the hand of Pharaoh (Ex. 3:1 – 4:17,21-23; 6:1-13).

This, I am convinced, is not dissimilar to Saul's conversion, and his being commissioned as an apostle by the Lord, charged to take the gospel to the Gentiles to bring them into liberty in Christ.[15] Paul himself saw his experience in that way. Hear him declaiming before Agrippa:

I was going to Damascus with the authority and commission of the chief priests. About noon, O king, as I was on the road, I saw a light from heaven, brighter than the sun, blazing around me and my companions. We all fell to the ground, and I heard a voice saying to me in Aramaic: 'Saul, Saul, why do you persecute me? It is hard for you to kick against the goads'. Then I asked: 'Who are you, Lord?'. 'I am Jesus, whom you are persecuting', the Lord replied. 'Now get up and stand on your feet. I have appeared to you to appoint you as a servant and as a witness of what you have seen of me and what I will show you. I will rescue you from your own people and from the Gentiles. I am sending you to them to open their eyes and turn them from darkness to light, and from the power of Satan to God, so that they may receive forgiveness of sins and a place among those who are sanctified by faith in me'. So then, King Agrippa, I was not disobedient to the vision from heaven (Acts 26:12-19).

Although it is blindingly obvious to say it, Paul was a converted Jew, and all his writings are steeped in Old Testament allusions;

---

[15] I am being cautious. The strict and full comparison (contrast – see my *Christ*) is between Moses and Christ (John 1:17).

steeped in them, I say. And not only allusions; in the apostle's writings, we meet an abundance of direct quotations from the Old Testament. No wonder, then, that Paul, describing his life and ministry, did so by means of old-covenant allusions (Rom. 15:16; Phil. 2:17; 2 Tim. 4:6).

Now, whatever else may be said about Moses and the LORD commissioning him to lead Israel out of bondage into liberty, 'unique' must surely spring to mind. Likewise for Paul.

So, getting back to Saul's conversion, I think we may safely deduce the following: whatever the three accounts tell us about the laying on of hands, it would at most be best to regard the episode as extraordinary, as the commissioning of an apostle. That being the case, it would surely be foolish – not to say, audacious – to use it to try to build a norm for church practice today. 'Pastors' are not Saul. And who claims to be Ananias?

Paul and Barnabas (Acts 13:1-3)
Once again, the relevant words:

In the church at Antioch there were prophets and teachers... While they were worshipping [ministered to, NKJV] the Lord and fasting, the Holy Spirit said: 'Set apart for me Barnabas and Saul for the work to which I have called them'. So, after they had fasted and prayed, they placed their hands on them, and sent them off (Acts 13:1-3).

Note Luke's use of the verb *leitourgeō*, to worship (minister, NKJV), and compare this with Romans 15:16.[16] Significantly, the Septuagint uses this word to describe the work of an old-covenant priest and a Levite, and Luke took it up it in Acts 13:2, bypassing the more usual *diakonos*. In this way, yet again, old-covenant overtones are evident – overtones such as the children of Israel laying hands on the Levites at their dedication to the Lord's service (Num. 8.10). Warkentin struck the right note:

The laying on of hands on these two [Paul and Barnabas] was neither to recognise gifts for leadership nor to commission them for service...

---

[16] Where Paul used *leitourgon*, minister, and *hierourgounta*, priestly duty ('ministering', NKJV).

Paul and Barnabas were setting out to mediate the new covenant to the peoples, both Jew and Gentile. They had priestly authority to do so.[17]

In other words, we have a further example of the epoch-making, extraordinary events Luke so often records in old-covenant terms. Consequently, as before, it would be unwise to try to make this extraordinary incident a norm for our practice today. Furthermore, the part of about 'the laying on of hands' is often adopted. What about the direct revelation from God the Holy Spirit? What about the 'prophets and teachers'? And so on. As I say, it would seem unwise, at the very least, to turn such an extraordinary event into a norm for today – especially when the selection from the original package has to be so selective.

So, to summarise the Acts passages which refer to the laying on of hands: Luke is concerned to show how the Spirit of God enabled the early church to take the gospel out to the world, in fulfilment of Acts 1:8. He does this by not only recording a series of volcanic events, but by drawing heavily upon old-covenant concepts and practices, and applying them to this unfolding, new-covenant realisation of God's purpose. While it has to be admitted that these allusions to the old covenant are more readily discerned in the Greek than in our English translations, they are there, all the same. Luke was describing extraordinary, epoch-making events, interventions or eruptions in the spread of the gospel in the early days of the new covenant.

Let me stress the 'extraordinary'. This major point, fully grasped, has enormous consequences; the laying on of hands in Acts must be seen in its light. To try to use these passages to establish church practice for us today is to force the passages into a mould for which they were not designed. It is to try to make them do something Luke never intended for them. As James Packer said on another, but not altogether unconnected, issue: 'I guess Luke would have been both startled and distressed had he foreseen how some of his latter-day readers would misconstrue him in these matters'.[18]

---

[17] Warkentin p134.
[18] Packer p205.

So much for the laying on of hands in Acts. Now for those three remaining references to it in the two letters to Timothy.

Laying on of hands in the Pastoral Letters[19]

And so we are reduced to the three remaining references to the laying on of hands, all of which are found in Paul's letters to Timothy. I will take 1 Timothy 4:14 and 2 Timothy 1:6 together, leaving consideration of 1 Timothy 5:22 to a separate section. In taking the first two together, I am making no comment either way as to whether or not they refer to the same event. I simply do not know. Whatever they may claim, nor does anybody else. This, in itself, is not without significance. In this matter, it is often easier to say what we do *not* know than what we do.

1 Timothy 4:14 and 2 Timothy 1:6
Paul commanded Timothy:

Do not neglect your gift, which was given you through a prophetic message when the body of elders laid their hands on you (1 Tim. 4:14). I remind you to fan into flame the gift of God, which is in you through the laying on of my hands (2 Tim. 1:6).

These are, perhaps, the key verses in this entire debate. It doesn't take an Einstein to work out what might be made of them – indeed, what *has* been made of them, and *is* made of them: when we (or rather, the proper, qualified ministers) lay hands on a man today, we (they) convey a gift to him. By this rite, the man in question is ordained to the ministry, and he, by having had hands laid upon him, has been gifted for that ordained ministry. He, in turn, now has the power to ordain other men. Quite a lot out of two verses! Is it a just conclusion? Is it safe?

Well... if this is indeed the proper deduction from the passages, then the laying on of hands truly is a sacrament; and, to boot, a sacrament of high order. So... let's get on with it! Let's ordain as many men as we can, men who will be specially set apart, gifted

---

[19] I feel I have little choice but to succumb to the usual designation for Paul's letters to Timothy and Titus, even though I am not at all sure it is the right way to describe them.

with far-reaching powers. Indeed, why stop at the sacramental? If we think it right to apply old-covenant principles to our practices under the new covenant, let us become fully-fledged sacerdotalists, and have done with it!

But before we get carried away with such an interpretation, with all the consequences that it entails, with all the turning-upside-down of the New Testament it necessitates, perhaps it would be sensible just to pause and ask a few questions.

For a start, note the 'you': 'given *you... * on *you... * in *you'*. Paul was talking to Timothy, obviously. But the question is: In this context are we to regard Timothy as an 'ordinary' man or an 'extraordinary'? In other words, was the apostle here addressing Timothy and reminding him of that time when, allowing the terminology for sake of argument, as an 'ordinary' ministerial candidate, about to be appointed as 'the pastor' at Ephesus, he (the apostle) laid hands on him and so was the means of imparting a gift to the younger man? Or was the apostle addressing Timothy as an extraordinary man, called to an extraordinary task, and who was extraordinarily gifted in an extraordinary way? Clearly, much hangs upon the alternative we choose. For my part, I have not the slightest hesitation in taking it in the latter way. As I have argued, the New Testament knows nothing of 'the pastor' of any church. Certainly, Timothy was not 'the pastor' of the church at Ephesus. All the evidence, as far as I can judge, points to Timothy and Titus being apostolic delegates. So much for the 'you'.

Then notice the 'my': '*my* hands'. Paul was speaking of his own hands, obviously. But was he speaking as an 'ordinary' man who had himself been ordained, and was now using his hands (and powers) to 'ordain' Timothy to turn him into a minister? Or was he speaking as an apostle – an extraordinary officer if ever there was one – and, as an apostle, laying his hands on an extraordinary man for an extraordinary occasion? Once again, large issues depend on the choice. As before, for my part, bearing in mind the rest of the New Testament, I have not the slightest hesitation in taking it in the latter way.

And what about 'the body of elders'? Who were they? And how were they connected with Paul in this affair? Were they connected with him? Or did they lay hands on Timothy on a separate occasion? Gill thought 'the body of elders' or 'eldership' (NKJV)[20] were the apostles, and he provided supporting arguments.[21] Was he right? I don't know. Can anybody be sure? It is a possibility. And if Paul *was* speaking about fellow-apostles, such an extraordinary episode ought to stop us making a sweeping application of it to our ordinary affairs.

At the very least, until categorical answers can be given to these questions, it would hardly be wise to rush into setting up a full-blown sacramental rite to turn men into ordained ministers, and to make its observance the standard practice in the ordination of 'the pastor' of a church; especially so, bearing in mind the silence of the New Testament on both the practice and 'the pastor'. Oh, I know that there is plenty of supporting evidence for both, and instruction on both, to be found in the Fathers, and in contemporary manuals of church life; but in the New Testament, there is not a whisper of it. Food for thought?

All that, I admit, is negative. But it is a necessary negative to serve as a corrective before we let ourselves be swept off our feet, and adopt a rite that, although it may have *prima facie* scriptural support, and has been 'justified' by centuries of tradition, is – in fact – pure Father-ism!

Now for the positive. Let me remind you of a point I have already made: although it is blindingly obvious to say it, Paul was a converted Jew, and all his writings are steeped in Old Testament allusions; steeped in them, I say. And not only allusions; in the apostle's writings, we meet an abundance of direct quotations from the Old Testament. Nowhere is all this more true than in these letters to Timothy. While this *modus operandi* stands out clearly enough in our English translations, it can be discerned even more strongly in the Greek, especially bearing in mind the apostle's use of the Septuagint. The fact is, in these particular letters, there are more than a score of such Old Testament allusions and references, including the Jewish father-son overtones in Paul's charges to Timothy. Take, for example, 1 Timothy 1:2,18; 4:6-16; 5:21; 6:11-12,20; 2 Timothy 1:5-8,13-14; 2:1-8,14; 4:5-8 – *passim* really. To my mind, this is highly suggestive. I go further. I think it is plain.

[20] 'The presbytery' (AV) is a loaded phrase nowadays.
[21] Gill: *Commentary* Vol.6 p609.

Moreover, Paul, versed in the Moses-Joshua relationship (Ex. 17:9-14; 24:13-14; 33:11; Num. 27:15-23; Deut. 31:23; see also Josh. 1; 3:7; 4:14; 8:34-35; 11:15, for instance – *passim*, really), addresses Timothy in that vein.[22] In these addresses, while I do not claim that the link-up is explicit or absolute, I am convinced it is there. Moses laid hands on Joshua (Num. 27:18,23; Deut. 34:9), commissioning him to his great work of taking Israel into the promised land.

In this light, Paul, having commissioned Timothy for his battle with the Judaisers and the Gnostics at Ephesus, now writes these two letters to him to put backbone into his apostolic delegate. The apostle is restless, concerned about him; over and over again, he does what he can to stiffen Timothy's resolve, charging him, reminding him of his own sufferings and determination, and so on (see both letters, *passim*). Conscious that he (Paul) is soon to die (2 Tim. 4:6-7), the apostle reminds the younger man of the Moses-Joshua like experience when he (Paul) had passed the responsibility on to Timothy. Timothy is the 'man of God' (1 Tim. 6:11), the man on the spot – God's man, the apostle's delegate, the man who has had the apostle's hands laid upon him. He must rise to the measure of events and play his part – he must! – just as Joshua did under the old covenant.

This, of course, means that the situation and the arrangements in question tend (to put it no stronger) to the extraordinary through and through. Paul was specially gifted. Of that there is no doubt. So was Timothy. The whole episode is special. Now whether this special event, concerning two special men, for specific and special circumstances, can be extrapolated to us and our routine affairs certainly merits serious and careful thought.

As for 'the body of elders', are we not reminded of Acts 13:1-3, and the way Paul and Barnabas were commissioned for their special work? If so, my remarks on that passage (which see) apply here.

Warkentin:

There is no hint that Paul attaches any significance other than the special endowment for office (after the model of Joshua) and the

---

[22] See Warkentin pp136-140.

sharing of his own unique commission, with the act of the imposition of hands... Paul calls Timothy a 'man of God' (1 Tim. 6:11), a term indicating prophetic office, and used of Moses (Deut. 33:1). Because this term has been appropriated by church leaders throughout history one must beware of automatically associating it with the pastoral office. Paul does not depict Timothy as the prototype of the pastor or elder... Rather, Paul places Timothy's office in a covenantal setting; if [that] historical context is stripped away, the office becomes vulnerable to manipulation.

Let me stress this. 'Because this term' – 'the man of God' – 'has been appropriated by church leaders throughout history one must beware of automatically associating it with the pastoral office'. This is a very important caveat or warning, one which is not always heeded. There is a very real danger – I am convinced it is a frequent occurrence – of reading back into the New Testament the Church-crustaceans which have accumulated during the long centuries of Christendom. This is a grievous imposition on Scripture, and it proves a most effective filter to keep us from seeing Scripture as it really is. By reading the Bible through Christendom's glasses, we merely confirm what may well be error – and often is error; at the very least, it may confirm unbiblical innovations which have been foisted on the gospel and the church. And of those, there are not a few!

Again, do not miss: 'if [that] historical context is stripped away'. This is a vital step down the slippery slope. Once the historical context is forgotten or ignored, the phrase, 'the man of God', becomes highly 'vulnerable to manipulation'. And how! Notice how the historical setting of Paul's use is indeed stripped away to let the phrase, 'the man of God', be bandied about today without regard for its biblical context. And the context is always paramount!

A glance at a concordance will confirm that 'the man of God' is used frequently in the Old Testament, but with singular discrimination. It is applied to Moses, to the angel of God, to a prophet, to Elijah and Elisha, for instance. As for the New Testament, the phrase 'man of God' is used only twice: in addition to 1 Timothy 6:11, it is used in 2 Timothy 3:17 – 'so that the man of God may be thoroughly equipped for every good work'. This could be general, yes, but note how the context here is heavily personal to Timothy himself. I do not say that the passage may not be applied to all believers, but the overwhelming evidence of Scripture is that 'the man of God' is not to be treated as a kind of ministerial confetti to be sprinkled willy-nilly over the man in the pulpit. How often this is done! It is often done, moreover, with the sinister effect – if not purpose – of distinguishing and separating 'the man of God' (in the pulpit) from the *hoi polloi* in the pew. The fact is, every believer – including every female believer – is 'a man of God', a competent minister of the new covenant (2 Cor. 3:6).[23]

To let Warkentin go on. Referring to: 'What you heard from me, keep as the pattern of sound teaching... Guard the good deposit that was entrusted to you – guard it with the help of the Holy Spirit who lives in us' (2 Tim. 1:13-14), she observed:

These are not generalised instructions for preaching the gospel, no matter how applicable they may appear for that purpose. The laying on of hands on Timothy is not a rite initiated by the apostolic church with a view to setting a normative pattern for induction into pastoral or missionary roles... Historically, Paul sets the imposition of hands on Timothy in the context of the entry of the Israelites into the land of Canaan (Deut. 32 – 34), and in that of his own commissioning for specific duty (Acts 13:1-3). By using the Moses-Joshua [scenario] and by linking Timothy's office to the levitical ordination through analogy with the laying on of hands on [surely a misprint – it should be 'of'] Paul, the writer of the Pastorals interprets the contemporary scene [that is, that which was going on at Ephesus at that time] for the people of God.[24]

All this would become more evident if the Moses-Joshua episode, and not that of Ananias-Saul, were made the norm for the ordination of 'the pastor' today. Perhaps, when ordaining their new pastor, not a few churches would be happy to think that they had

---

[23] While the New Testament does occasionally distinguish 'the minister' – better 'the servant' – it does so in a very different way to what is virtually ubiquitous today. As I have said elsewhere: 'We should never forget that the best of teachers are but men, *only* ministers. As Paul put it: "Who then is Paul, and who is Apollos, *but* ministers...?" (1 Cor. 3:5, NKJV). Do not miss the "but"! The NIV is even more blunt: "What, after all, is Apollos? And what is Paul? Only servants...". Only! Do not miss the "only"!' (Gay: *Pastor* p46).
[24] Warkentin pp142-143. See also Kent pp164-165.

been favoured by a visiting Moses who had just ordained their new Joshua for them!

If that last remark of mine is too subtle for some, let me take the wraps off. The point I am making certainly merits it, and since I do not want it to be missed, I will be blunt. Rome did not develop the Papacy for nothing. Men hanker after a priest; indeed, men hanker after a pope: men like to be told what is what. Notice I said 'men'; I did not say 'papists'. Popery is not confined to Rome, alas. The desire for sacerdotal authority is endemic, I am afraid. Sad to say, it is not unknown among evangelicals and the Reformed. Howls of anguished disbelief and anger may rise, but I stand by my words. Oh, such men are not called 'popes'; of course not. Nevertheless, how nice it is, how pleasant it is, how handy it is – or so many think – to have a qualified man who can explain it all to us!

'Who thinks and talks like this among the evangelicals and the Reformed?' Do I hear the question? I can only speak for myself, of course, but I detect plenty of evidence that this kind of 'popery' lies not so very far beneath the surface. If evidence is required, please see my previous works on the theme. Many really do look upon their 'pastor' as the fount of all wisdom, the one who authoritatively defines the meaning of the Bible for them, the arbiter of all their difficult decisions, and the confessor figure for all their wrongs; in short, their 'pope'. I said I would be blunt! There is need.[25]

---

[25] See my *Christ* p403. I quote the closing section of the relevant extract: 'Whether it is Rome, the Reformed, Baptists or Uncle Tom Cobley, while, in our darkness, we make proper use of the candles other men have left behind, unless Scripture is paramount, in reality as well as in slogan, we are nothing but papists of one shade or another. "Give us a pope to tell us what to believe!" There are far more popes about than that aged gentleman who lives in the Vatican, and there are more papal bulls in circulation than evangelicals and the Reformed usually admit. And those bulls aren't all issued at Rome! It is altogether too possible to turn the Westminster, the 1689, or whatever, into a papal pronouncement, set in stone, untouchable *and all-authoritative*'. See also my *Pastor* pp113,226,264,270,314, for instance. See my earlier note on 'the leading brother' who had 'all the truth'. By the way, that incident was far from

Incidentally, is it not worthy of note that when the time came, Joshua did not see fit to designate a successor? This, to my mind, clearly underscores the extraordinary circumstances surrounding the first relationship. And Timothy certainly never appointed a successor as apostolic delegate. Elders and teachers had to be recognised and charged, yes (2 Tim. 2:2), but there is not the slightest whiff in Scripture of 'apostolic succession' – which corrosive invention, by the way, makes its appearance in various and (shall we say) more acceptable guises – yes, even among Nonconformists!

The point is, in the Pastoral letters we are talking about something which is clearly extraordinary, applicable only to Timothy (and Paul).[26] It is quite wrong to force Paul's words into a generalised application to 'ministers' or 'the pastor'.

Sadly, Bible teachers and commentators have not always seen it this way. Take Donald Guthrie, who surely overstepped the mark when he generalised his comments on 2 Timothy 1:6, saying: 'Every Christian minister needs at times to return to the inspiration of his ordination, to be reminded... of the adequacy of the divine grace which enables him to perform [his ministry]'.[27] It is not difficult to see what that kind of unwarranted talk might lead to.

---

isolated; there were repeated instances of that man acting authoritatively, lording it over men's faith – and other matters!

[26] Note the way the apostle concluded this charge to Timothy: 'What you heard from me, keep as the pattern of sound teaching... Guard the good deposit that was entrusted to you – guard it with the help of the Holy Spirit who lives in us' (2 Tim. 1:13-14). The Holy Spirit, Paul might have said, dwells in *you*. But, linking himself with Timothy, he spoke of 'us'. Paul, as it were, was with his delegate at Ephesus, with him heart and soul. Is it a step too far to apply the apostle's words to the Corinthians to the situation? 'Even though I am not physically present, I am with you in spirit. And I have already passed judgment on the one who did this, just as if I were present. When you are assembled in the name of our Lord Jesus and I am with you in spirit, and the power of our Lord Jesus is present...' (1 Cor. 5:3-4). As for 2 Tim. 1:13-14, I realise, of course, that the Spirit indwells all believers, but in the context of the Pastoral letters it is possible that the apostle was confining his remarks to himself and Timothy. I put this tentative suggestion forward for consideration, that is all.

[27] Guthrie p126.

And take Handley Moule. Having assumed that the two Timothy passages coincide, and they refer to 'Timothy's Ordination to the ministerial office', and Richard Hooker's talk of 'the holy Sacraments', Moule came to application:

> May Ordination to the ministry of Christ in his Church today be, by the man who bears it, ever viewed, and ever used, as... Paul bade his son in the faith view and use his Ordination then. So ministry will be a ministry of power indeed.[28]

Will it?

And Calvin, in words I have already quoted:

> Paul... here speaks of ordination; that is, of the solemn act of conferring [note the word] the office of the ministry... I think... that Paul here speaks of the office of a pastor.[29]

Let C.H.Spurgeon bring us back (almost) to scriptural reality. I say 'almost', because he begged the question on a couple of occasions. I quote some of what he said when preaching 2 Timothy 1:6:

> Paul... speaks of the gift that was conferred by the laying on of his hands, and in the former letter he connects that with the hands of the presbytery. Now, it was no doubt[?!] the custom to lay hands at the ordination[30] of Christian ministers by the apostles, and there was an excellent reason for it, for gifts were thereby conveyed to the ordained, and when we can find anybody who can thereby confer some spiritual gift upon us, we shall be glad to have their hands laid on our heads; but empty hands we care not for. Rites cease when their meaning ceases. If practiced any longer they gender to superstition, and are instruments of priestcraft. The upholding of the hands of the eldership, when they give their vote to elect a man to the pastorate,[31] is a sensible proceeding; and is, I suspect, all the apostle means when he speaks of the presbytery;[32] but empty hands it seems to me are fitly laid on empty heads, and to submit to an empty ceremony is the idlest

---

[28] Moule pp46-48. I have deliberately retained Moule's use of capitals.
[29] Calvin: *Commentaries* Vol.21 Part 3 pp189-190.
[30] Spurgeon was here begging the question as to the meaning of 'ordination'.
[31] Once again, Spurgeon was begging a very important question.
[32] Spurgeon was wide of the mark here, reading back into the New Testament the inventions of the Fathers and the settled mistaken practice of the following centuries.

of all idle waste of time.[33] If Paul were here, and could confer a gift, we should rejoice to receive it; indeed, and if the [lowliest] man in Christendom, or woman either, could confer the smallest drachma of grace by the putting on of their hands, we would bow our head in the lowliest manner; till then we shall beg to decline submitting to the imposition, or assisting in it.[34]

For my part, in the main thrust of what he said here, I am with Spurgeon and not Guthrie, Moule and Calvin on this issue. How about you, reader?

To those who prefer the latter, may I issue a warning? You will have to guard, and guard with exceeding care, against allowing sacramental and sacerdotal ideas to flourish among the ministers and the people. Just a minute! Did you spot it, reader? Did you spot the deliberate – but grossly unbiblical – distinction I just made between 'the ministers'; and 'the people'? This, you see, is precisely what I am talking about. These sacerdotal ideas, so small at first, creep in unawares. So I say it again, if you do adopt the view put forward by Guthrie, Moule and Calvin, you will have to be ever-watchful. You will find the struggle uphill all the way, and, I fear, the struggle will prove too much; I am afraid that history is against you being able to fend off the sacerdotal. 'All roads lead to Rome'.[35] The notion may start off as seemingly benign, but I fear it will eventually end at Rome. Alarmist? I say two things in reply: history provides plenty of evidence of it; and time will tell.

And so we come to our final text.

1 Timothy 5:22

Paul commanded Timothy:

I charge you, in the sight of God and Christ Jesus and the elect angels... do not be hasty in the laying on of hands, and do not share in the sins of others. Keep yourself pure (1 Tim. 5:21-22).

---

[33] Worse. It is, in fact, the cause of immense mischief!

[34] Spurgeon: *Metropolitan* pp625-626.

[35] '*Mille viae ducunt homines per saecula Romam* (A thousand roads lead men forever to Rome) in *Liber Parabolarum*, 591 (1175), by Alain de Lille. The earliest English form appears to be: "Right as various paths lead the folk the right way to Rome" (Geoffrey Chaucer)' (modernised from Wikipedia).

From the time of Chrysostom (c347-407), men have viewed 1 Timothy 5: 22 as evidence for ordination by means of the laying on of hands. As Warkentin observed: 'Thus the meaning of the text was shaped early in Church history by connecting it to a sacramental view of the laying on of hands in ordination'. It was, indeed, set in concrete, and did nothing to prevent the rise and spread of sacerdotalism. As Warkentin further noted:

This text is thus still frequently taken to refer to ordination... Even though 1 Timothy 5:22 is noted for its difficulty, Chrysostom's interpretation is often taken as though the meaning is straightforward.[36]

She was right. Let me prove it.

Take Homer Kent commenting on the verse: 'The laying on of hands is known with certainty to have been used in the ordination of elders'.[37] Is it?

Take William Hendriksen who likewise assumed Chrysostom's reading: 'Much trouble can be avoided if in the matter of ordaining men to office Timothy will exercise the necessary precaution: "Do not lay hands (of ordination) upon anyone hastily..."'. True, Hendriksen spoke in terms of 'the symbolical indication of the impartation of gifts',[38] but the damage had been done. In his opinion, was the candidate gifted before the ordination rite, or not? If he was, why do it? If not, then there is nothing symbolic about it – ordination by the laying on of hands is entirely effective; in other words, ordination is a powerful – immensely powerful – sacrament. In any case, as I have said, it is what people imagine to be going on which counts, not the theological niceties. When they witness hands being laid on the man who is to become their 'pastor', they have no doubts that something has happened to him to fit him for the job; coupled with incessant ministerial language, the thing is a *fait accompli*.

Calvin had no doubts about the meaning of the verse: 'The laying on of hands means ordination; that is, the sign is put for the

---

[36] Warkentin p144.
[37] Kent p187.
[38] Hendriksen p185. See also Guthrie p107.

thing signified... to receive into the ministerial office'.[39] The same goes for many others. Take R.Martin Pope: 'The act of ordination is meant'.[40] Take J.H.Bernard: 'The [Anglican] Church has sanctioned the interpretation of the words which refers them to ordination, by embodying them in the Ember Collect'. Bernard rightly dismissed the notion that the reference might be to the receiving back into the fold of repentant presbyters after they had sinned, saying: 'There is no evidence that it was accustomed usage in apostolic times nor is [the word] or any similar phrase used in such a context elsewhere in the New Testament'.[41] Quite. But the same could be said of ordination to ministerial office!

In his turn, even Gill sailed close to the wind. He thought the apostle was speaking of:

The admission of persons into the work of the ministry, and installing of them into the office of an elder or pastor... Do not hastily and at once admit any person into the sacred work of the ministry, or constitute him an elder, or pastor, over a church of Christ.[42]

Begging a few questions here, I think!

Let us come to the verse. The truth is, the text is fraught with difficulties of interpretation; it has proved to be a veritable minefield – or graveyard – for interpretations! Unfortunately, it has not proved a graveyard for the usual 'ministerial ordination' view; quite the reverse, as I have shown!

As for the difficulties, take the context, for one thing; the paragraph division, for another. What about the connection of the verse with the preceding verse and/or the one which follows? Due weight is not always given to Paul's 'I solemnly charge' (1 Tim. 5:21, NASB).[43] Even more damaging than the work of Bible commentators, Bible translators often simply assume Chrysostom's interpretation, and fit their translation into his

---

[39] Calvin: *Commentaries* Vol.21 Part 3 p145.
[40] Pope p113.
[41] Bernard pp87-88.
[42] Gill: *Commentary* Vol.6 p616.
[43] In 1 Tim. 5:21; 2 Tim. 2:14; 4:1, Paul uses *diamarturomai*, 'to testify earnestly' with the idea of 'solemnly affirm'. In 1 Tim. 6:13, Paul uses *paraggellō*, 'to declare, announce, command, order'. See Thayer.

template. As we have seen, the reading-back (by translators as well as commentators) of modern sentiments into the text is far from uncommon. It is the norm! Again, the translation: 'Lay hands... on no *man*' (AV), 'do not lay hands on *anyone*' (NKJV, NASB), carries risk. The masculine 'man' or 'any*one*' is nearly always assumed, instead of the perfectly possible neuter 'any*thing*'. But is it 'lay hands on' no 'one' or no 'thing'? The NIV avoided the problem!

And so on and on. The truth is, nobody can be definite even as to the exact meaning of 'lay hands on'! We just cannot assume it means what it commonly means today – and has meant since the time of the Fathers. One of our greatest dangers is to read the Bible through 1800 years of Christendom. Forgive my harping on about it, but it is the sad reality – and it is a very, very serious mistake indeed. It is the source of much of our present trouble in this area.

In light of all these difficulties, it would seem advisable to let caution keep us from wild leaps of speculation which can only lead us to the setting-up of such a powerful rite for which the New Testament affords no clear-cut basis.

Let Warkentin summarise all this: 'Whatever the interpretation of 1 Timothy 5:22, it is evident that this text cannot be used to buttress any argument for the laying on of hands in ordination to church office'. Extending her comments to both letters to Timothy, Warkentin went on:

To claim that 1 and 2 Timothy offer a 'clear picture of Christian ordination as it was adopted by the Pauline churches from the Jewish-Christian church in Palestine' is manifestly a mis-statement [it is a gross over-statement]. The [grievous] power of the unquestioned assumptions underlying this assertion has been apparent throughout the history of the church. The mark of such thinking has been felt in our [Bible] translations, and has thus been perpetuated throughout the rank and file of Christianity. The person who does not know the biblical languages is dependent on the care, skill and integrity of those who have translated the version he or she uses. For those who insist on the authority of the Scriptures, such misleading translations are not to be lightly dismissed as of little consequence.[44]

---

[44] Warkentin pp151-152.

In short, having looked at all the relevant passages in Acts and the letters to Timothy, I cannot see how a cogent case can be made from the New Testament for the laying on of hands today.

Jesus Christ... has made us to be a kingdom and priests to serve his God and Father

Revelation 1:5-6

Conclusion

I closed the previous chapter by saying that I fail to see how a cogent case can be made from the New Testament for the laying on of hands today. And the notion of ordaining a man to be 'a minister', 'a pastor', a clergyman or whatever, is, of course, quite foreign – contrary, indeed – to the new-covenant doctrine of the priesthood of all believers, those believers having, all of them, been 'ordained to the ministry' at their conversion.[1] Putting these two together, it is not surprising, therefore to find no New Testament warrant for the practice of the laying on of hands in ordination to the ministry.

Consequently, since we lack this New Testament warrant, and because of the dangers so glaringly inherent in the practice of ordination, dangers which are so easily exacerbated when attended by the rite of the laying on of hands – namely sacramentalism and sacerdotalism – we should have no truck with either ordination or the laying on of hands.

Marjorie Warkentin:

The events of the new [covenant] age in which the imposition of hands occur are unique, once-for-all situations. The laying on of hands has nothing to do with routine installation into office in the church, whether as elder, deacon, pastor or missionary. Rather, that action confirmed to the new [covenant] people of God [the new Israel] that Yahweh, the God of the covenant, was even now faithfully implementing the fulfilment of his covenant promises to his people...

The doctrine of ordination has been beset by arguments from silence and the selective use of texts. The church, with a quite natural concern to maintain order and preserve lines of authority, has, at times, seemed to have a greater commitment to stability of the *status quo* than to the primacy of taking the gospel to the ends of the earth...

The creation of a privileged class of believers presents a danger to the priesthood of all believers... When the Spirit of God 'lays hands on' men and women at conversion, this is their consecration, their call to serve their high priest, Jesus Christ. They become members of the royal priesthood; they are the Levites of the new covenant. God has

---

[1] For my reasons, see my *Priesthood*; *Pastor*.

made provision for their ordination at [conversion].[2] They need no other.[3]

Indeed, it all boils down to the burden of my *The Pastor: Does He Exist?* As I have said: 'All roads lead to Rome'. I am afraid that in this matter, the proverb is only too true. In all these shenanigans connected with ordaining a man to make him 'a minister', thus moving him out of the New Testament ministerial-class of all believers into a 'special' class of Ministers – the clergy[4] – there is one great casualty: the person and work of the Lord Jesus Christ. As soon as we begin to elevate a man – for whatever reason, and in whatever way – the inevitable consequence is a degrading of Christ.

Is that doubted? The proof is easy. Because the exaltation of men and the cultivation of cliques and factions were rampant problems at Corinth, Paul devoted a great deal of space in his first letter to put a stop to them. And how! See 1 Corinthians 1:10-17; 3:1 – 4:21 for a start. He pulled no punches. And what was his main point? The glory of Christ! Opening his case with an appeal: 'I appeal to you, brothers, in the name of our Lord Jesus Christ' (1 Cor. 1:10), he was soon taking the Corinthians to Christ... Christ... Christ. Setting out argument after argument, the apostle thundered:

Christ Jesus... has become for us wisdom from God – that is, our righteousness, holiness and redemption. Therefore, as it is written: 'Let him who boasts boast in the Lord'... I resolved to know nothing while I was with you except Jesus Christ and him crucified... We have the mind of Christ... No one can lay any foundation other than the one already laid, which is Jesus Christ... So then, no more boasting about men! All things are yours, whether Paul or Apollos or Cephas or the world or life or death or the present or the future – all are yours, and you are of Christ, and Christ is of God (1 Cor. 1:30-31; 2:2,16; 3:11,21-23).

---

[2] Sadly, Warkentin had 'baptism', pure Luther. She was much closer to the biblical position with: 'The general call to the ministry issued to all the elect of God at salvation' (Warkentin p60). I prefer 'conversion'.
[3] Warkentin pp156,176,181,188; she was quoting Eduard Lohse.
[4] Even though the word may not be used, 'clergy' *is* what we are talking about; see my *Pastor*.

Conclusion

I think the case is made: as we boast about men, or look to men, we inevitably lower Christ.

The true pastor and priest of the souls of men is none other than the Lord Jesus Christ himself. Consequently, let us shun anything and everything that in any way detracts from his glory and his uniqueness, and takes the smallest step towards obscuring Christ and exalting man. In this instance, therefore, let us have nothing to do with the laying on of hands in ordination.

Of course, let us recognise, respect and honour our teachers and rulers in the churches. Yes, indeed; they are precious gifts of Christ to us. But in respecting such men, and in making new-covenant use of them, let us make sure that we never stray an inch towards sacramentalism and sacerdotalism. Among believers, there is no special class in the new covenant – except Christ! Christ alone is the true and great high priest. Under Christ, and in Christ, all believers are true ministers, all believers are true spiritual priests of the Lord, all offer true spiritual sacrifices. The elders in the churches are no more 'ministerial' than any and every member of Christ, and all of us – elders included – should never forget it. Indeed, the encouraging of the full realisation of the priesthood of all believers should be a high priority in our church life.

In short, apart from Christ: no sacerdotalism!

Therefore let us take the Lord Jesus Christ, let us take the Lord Jesus Christ alone, let us take him as our pastor (1 Pet. 2:25), as our priest and sacrifice (Heb. 4:14 – 5:10; 6:20 – 10:39; 13:10-15,20-21). We need no other; there is no other.

Reader, I hope the following words, by Charitie L.Bancroft, represent what you know to be the truth, and what you have come to feel in your heart. If they do not, I plead with you to make them your own. Call on the name of the Lord and you will be saved (Rom. 10:13). And this is what is involved in 'calling on Christ': you need a priest and a blood sacrifice to bring you to God. There is such a priest and sacrifice, but only one: the Lord Jesus Christ. Do not, I urge you, rest until you can truly echo these words:

Before the throne of God above
I have a strong and perfect plea.
A great high priest whose name is love
Who ever lives and pleads for me.

My name is graven on his hands,
My name is written on his heart.
I know that while in heaven he stands[5]
No tongue can bid me thence depart.

When Satan tempts me to despair
And tells me of the guilt within,
Upward I look and see him there
Who made an end of all my sin.

Because the sinless Saviour died
My sinful soul is counted free.
For God the just is satisfied
To look on him and pardon me.

Behold him there! the risen Lamb!
My perfect spotless righteousness,
The great unchangeable I AM,
The King of glory and of grace.

One with himself I cannot die.
My soul is purchased by his blood,
My life is hid with Christ on high,
With Christ my Saviour and my God!

In conclusion, if I may be permitted a little versifying[6] of my own:

Look I to a man who has been 'ordained'
To serve as my 'priest' – whatever his name?
No! I set my heart on Christ Jesus alone –
The Lord my Redeemer, my priest on his throne.

---

[5] Would Charitie have preferred 'appears', but poetic licence, the need for rhyme, and all that? The truth is, Christ now sits. But, let us not forget, Christ stood to receive Stephen (Acts 7:55-56).

[6] Despite Spurgeon's rebuking comment: 'Many of you have no doubt versified a little (as which of us in some weak moment has not?)' (Spurgeon: 'Faculty' p154).

Source List

Bernard, J.H.: *Cambridge Greek Testament for Schools – The Pastoral Epistles*, The University Press, Cambridge, 1899.

Calvin, John: *Institutes of the Christian Religion*, James Clarke & Co., Limited, London, 1957.

Calvin, John: *Commentaries*, Baker Book House, Grand Rapids, 1979.

Chadwick, Henry: *The Early Church*, Penguin Books, 1967.

Gill, John: *Gill's Commentary*, Baker Book House, Grand Rapids, 1980.

Gill, John: *A Complete Body of Doctrinal and Practical Divinity; or A System of Evangelical Truths, Deduced from the Sacred Scriptures*, Vol.3, W.Winterbotham, London, 1796.

Guthrie, Donald: *The Pastoral Epistles...*, The Tyndale Press, London, 1957.

Hendriksen, William: *The Epistles to Timothy and Titus*, The Banner of Truth Trust, London, 1959.

Kent, Homer A.: *The Pastoral Epistles...*, Moody Press, Chicago, 1958.

Moule, Handley C.G.: *The Second Epistle to Timothy...*, The Religious Tract Society, London, 1906.

Packer, J.I.: *Keep in Step with the Spirit*, Inter-Varsity Press, Leicester, 1984.

Pink, Arthur W.: *An Exposition of Hebrews*, Baker Book House, Grand Rapids, 1979.

Pope, R.Martin: *The Epistles of Paul the Apostle to Timothy and Titus...*, Charles H.Kelly, London, 1901.

Schaff, Philip: *History of the Christian Church, Vol.3: Nicene and Post-Nicene Christianity... 311-590*, Hendrickson, Peabody, 1996

Spurgeon, C.H.: *The Metropolitan Tabernacle Pulpit*, Vol.18, Passmore & Alabaster, London, 1873.

Spurgeon, C.H.: 'The Faculty of Impromptu Speech', *First Series of Lectures to my Students...*, Passmore and Alabaster, London, 1875.

Thayer, Joseph Henry: *A Greek-English Lexicon of the New Testament*, Baker Book House, Grand Rapids, Ninth Printing 1991.

Warkentin, Marjorie: *Ordination: A Biblical-Historical View*, Eerdmans, Grand Rapids, 1982.

Made in the USA
Middletown, DE
12 March 2022